World in Focus
Australia

OTTO JAMES

WAYLAND

First published in 2007 by Wayland

Copyright © Wayland 2007

Wayland
338 Euston Road, London NW1 3BH

Wayland Australia
Hachette Children's Books
Level 17/207 Kent Street
Sydney, NSW 2000

Commissioning editor: Nicola Edwards
Editor: Patience Coster
Inside design: Chris Halls, www.mindseyedesign.co.uk
Cover design: Wayland
Series concept and project management by EASI-Educational Resourcing
(info@easi-er.co.uk)
Statistical research: Anna Bowden
Maps and graphs: Martin Darlison, Encompass Graphics

Printed and bound in China

British Library Cataloguing in Publication Data
James, Otto
    Australia. - (World in focus)
    1. Australia - Juvenile literature
    I. Title
    994'.07

ISBN: 9780750247429

Cover top: The Bungle Bungles are a maze of narrow gorges and secluded gullies, rich in Aboriginal culture and history.
Cover bottom: Sydney Opera House is one of Australia's most popular tourist destinations.
Title page: Tourists admire the view from the edge of the Blue Mountains escarpment in New South Wales.

The author and publisher would like to thank the following for allowing their pictures to be reproduced in this publication:
Chris Fairclough Worldwide/Chris Fairclough 14, 19, 31, 42, 55; Corbis 8 (Frans Lanting), 9 (Swim Ink 2, LLC), 10 (Historical Picture Archive), 12 (Bettmann), 13 (Bettmann), 17 (Jon Jones/Sygma), 22 (Paul A Souders), 23 (David Gray/Reuters), 24 (Will Burgess/Pool/epa), 26 (David Austen/zefa), 27 (David G Houser/Post-Houserstock), 30 (Paul A Souders), 33 (Tim Wimborne/Reuters), 34 (Hulton-Deutsch Collection), 36 (Reuters), 38 (William Caram), 41 (Mick Tsikas/epa), 45 (Robert Garvey), 46 (Reuters), 47 (Reuters), 48 (Alberto Estevez/epa), 49 (Duomo), 50 (Franz-Marc Frei), *cover top* and 57 (Barry Lewis), 58 (STR/epa); EASI-Images (Rob Bowden) *cover bottom*, 4, 5, *title page* and 15, 16, 18, 20, 25, 29, 32, 35, 39, 40, 43, 51, 52, 53, 54, 56, 59; EASI-Images (Dawne Fahey) 6, 21, 28, 37, 44; Topfoto 11 (HIP).

The directional arrow portrayed on the map on page 7 provides only an approximation of north.

The data used to produce the graphics and data panels in this title were the latest available at the time of production.

CONTENTS

CHAPTER 1

Australia – An Overview

Australia occupies a giant island in the Southern Hemisphere, located between the South Pacific Ocean and the Indian Ocean. For tens of thousands of years this island was isolated from the rest of the world by the vast seas surrounding it. Australian plants and animals developed in their own, often distinctive, ways. The native Australians, known today as Indigenous Australian people, also developed their own unique way of life.

BRITISH SETTLERS

Australia only began to be settled by people from elsewhere in the world in the late-eighteenth century. In 1788, the first British settlers landed in a group of ships now known as the 'First Fleet'.

Until the twentieth century, Australia's different regions were separate: they only became linked together as one country in 1901.

Although Australia is geologically very old, it is a relatively young country in terms of the age of its people. During the twentieth century the population grew rapidly, mainly as a result of the immigration of young people from other parts of the world. Perhaps this is the reason why many Australians have a youthful, optimistic outlook on life.

▼ Sydney Harbour Bridge is one of Australia's most famous landmarks. This night view of Sydney also shows the Opera House on the left in the background.

► People go about their business in a busy shopping street near the Queen Victoria Building in Sydney. Many recent immigrants to Australia have come from an Asian background, especially from South-east Asian countries such as Korea and Vietnam. Others have come from troubled regions such as Kosovo and Afghanistan.

WHERE PEOPLE LIVE

All the major settlements in Australia are coastal cities. The interior cannot support large numbers of people because it is mainly hot, arid desert, which people find too harsh an environment to live in. Nine out of every ten Australians live in cities or urban areas. This is a higher proportion than in most other countries (in the year 2000, only 11 other countries had 90 per cent of their people living in urban areas).

Australian cities – especially the largest ones such as Sydney and Melbourne – have become increasingly multicultural since the 1950s. Many of the most recent immigrants to Australia have come from Asia. Earlier arrivals included people from the UK, Italy, Poland, Greece, and elsewhere in Europe, and Lebanon. In the less multicultural rural areas, most people are descended from British immigrants.

 Did you know?

About 1,500 different kinds of fish live on the Great Barrier Reef.

Focus on: The Great Barrier Reef

Lying off the north-east coast of Australia is one of the wonders of the natural world: the Great Barrier Reef. This is the largest coral reef in the world, stretching for over 2,000 km (1,200 miles). Diving or snorkelling trips to its shallow waters are one of Australia's most popular tourist attractions. People come to see the huge variety of animals living here, ranging from the tiny coral polyps that the reef is composed of, to sea turtles and great white sharks.

professionals and today number among high-profile judges, doctors, actors and athletes.

THE OUTBACK

The image many people have in mind when they think of Australia is of the Outback, or the 'Red Centre'. Here red soils, blue skies and sparse water supplies make for a beautiful but harsh environment, and amazing rock formations occasionally break up the flat landscape.

Much of Australia's early wealth depended on resources available in the Outback. Mineral wealth lies under the surface of many areas: gold, opals, iron and other ores are mined and sold abroad. At the fringes of the Outback lie lands that can be used for agriculture. Although not generally suited to arable farming this land is fine for keeping sheep, as they can survive by grazing the sparse vegetation. Parts of the Outback have giant sheep stations producing wool and meat for export.

▲ An abandoned tractor rests rusting on cattle-grazing land between the opal fields of Lightning Ridge and Sheepyard Mine in the Australian Outback of New South Wales.

INDIGENOUS AUSTRALIANS

Indigenous Australians are made up of two groups: Aborigines, who originally lived on the mainland, and Torres Strait Islanders, who originally came from the islands north of Australia. There also used to be an Indigenous Australian population in Tasmania. Wherever they live, be it rural or urban, Indigenous Australians are generally worse off than other Australians. They tend to live in worse housing, do less well at school, miss out on job opportunities and have shorter lives. They are Australia's poorest people, and were not given the same rights as other Australians until the 1960s. Even so, some Indigenous Australian people have become very successful

Physical geography

- Land area: 7,617,930 sq km/2,941,286 sq miles
- Water area: 68,920 sq km/26,610 sq miles
- Total area: 7,686,850 sq km/2,967,896 sq miles
- World rank (by area): 6
- Land boundaries: 0 km/0 miles
- Border countries: None
- Coastline: 25,760 km/16,007 miles
- Highest point: Mount Kosciuszko (2,229 m/7,313 ft)
- Lowest point: Lake Eyre (-15 m/-49 ft)

Source: CIA World Factbook

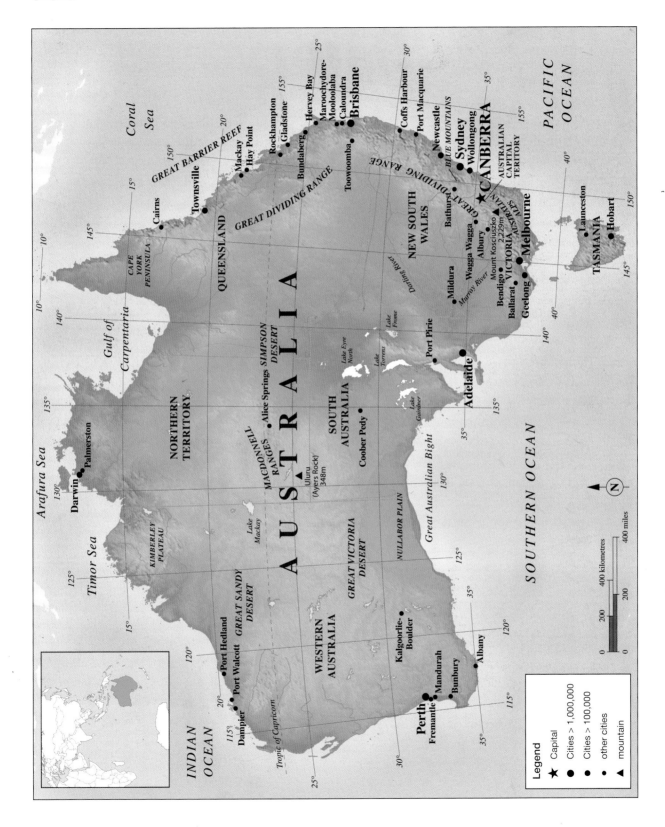

CHAPTER 2

History

Australian history dates back 65,000 years, to when Indigenous Australians arrived on the continent from Asia. Some experts believe that their arrival dates from only 40,000 years ago, but either way Indigenous Australians have been living in Australia for a very long time!

LIVING WITH THE LAND

The Indigenous Australians settled across most of the continent, including the interior. They developed a way of life that allowed them to cope with the harsh environment. Indigenous Australians lived in kinship groups, and for thousands of years their way of life continued without interruption from the outside world. During this time, the climate gradually became drier, wetter and then drier again. Indigenous Australian populations shrank or grew as the climate changed. In the driest periods there was not enough food and water for large numbers of people to survive, but in the wetter periods more people were able to live off the land. By the time the First Fleet arrived in Australia in 1788, there were probably about 750,000 Indigenous Australian people living across the continent. It is often assumed that the Indigenous Australians lived only in the hot desert areas, but they also lived on the coasts and in the colder areas to the south. For example, Tasmania, an island off Australia's south coast, had a large population of Indigenous Australians.

EUROPEAN EXPLORERS

Australia's name comes from the Latin word *australis*, which means 'southern'. For centuries, Europeans had spoken of *Terra Australis Incognita* – the 'Unknown Southern Land' – but there was no proof that this mythical place existed. Then, in 1606, a Dutch navigator called Willem Jansz sighted Cape York Peninsula in the far north-east of Australia, in what is now the state of Queensland.

◀ Aboriginal artist Turkey Tolson Tjupurrula at work in the Central Desert in Australia's Northern Territory. Many Indigenous Australian artists use a style of painting that has been handed down through the generations.

THE LANDING OF CAPTAIN COOK AT BOTANY BAY 1770

AUSTRALIA

▶ Captain Cook's arrival at Botany Bay is shown on an Australian tourism poster of the 1930s.

Between 1616 and 1636, Dutch navigators explored Australia's west, south-west and north-west coasts, but did not try to settle in the land they called 'New Holland'. In 1770, Captain James Cook of the British navy sighted and explored the fertile east coast of Australia. He claimed the region for Britain and called it New South Wales. This began Britain's acquisition of the whole continent.

'TRANSPORTATION'

In 1787, to relieve the overcrowding in its prisons, Britain began shipping convicts to prison colonies in New South Wales, in a practice known as 'transportation'. In 1788, eleven ships carrying around 730 convicts arrived in Botany Bay on the east coast. This was the First Fleet. Members of the fleet established a base about 11 km (7 miles) north of Botany Bay, which was eventually to become the city of Sydney.

? Did you know?

The boomerang is a traditional Indigenous Australian hunting weapon.

Focus on: Indigenous Australians

In 1788, there were roughly 500 different Indigenous Australian groups, each speaking its own language and each with strong ties to a particular area of land. Many Indigenous Australian myths and religious beliefs were linked to the land on which the people lived, with stories about almost every rock, stream, path or other feature of the landscape. Each group was made up in turn of small bands of people whose home was in a particular area. These bands rarely left 'their' area, because trespassing on another band's territory could end in violence.

During the 1790s, the British colonial government allowed military officers and freed convicts to begin settling their own lands. Free immigrants also began to arrive from Britain. Other colonial settlements followed, including Tasmania in 1803, Western Australia in 1829, South Australia in 1836, Victoria in 1851 and Queensland in 1859. The Northern Territory was established as a part of South Australia in 1863. In 1868, the British government finally abolished the practice of transportation.

EUROPEANS AND INDIGENOUS AUSTRALIANS

The arrival of the Europeans was a disaster for Indigenous Australians across Australia. The settlers brought diseases, such as influenza and smallpox, to which the Indigenous Australians had no resistance, and many died as a result. Others were expelled from the land their people had occupied for thousands of years. Some Indigenous Australian leaders resisted the European settlers. In the late 1700s and early 1800s, warriors such as Pemulwy, Dundalli and Jandamarra (also called Pigeon) tried to fight against the European invasion of their lands. But there was little they could do to stop the ever-increasing numbers of settlers. By the mid-1800s, the European settlers had erased all trace of traditional Indigenous Australian lifestyle from Tasmania.

THE WOOL TRADE

During the 1820s, settlers in New South Wales started to export wool back to Britain. This lucrative trade formed the basis for a strong economy, and increasing numbers of settlers decided to become sheep farmers. During the 1830s, some farmers moved from Tasmania and the area around Sydney to the rich grazing lands in southern New South Wales, thus founding the city of Melbourne. The settlers asked the British government for permission to make them a separate colony. In 1851, the area south of the Murray River became known as the colony of Victoria.

◀ A Gold Rush prospector, photographed in Queensland in 1867. The Gold Rush brought new citizens to Australia. Some of these people remained because they had failed to find gold and could not afford their passage home!

In 1851, gold was found in New South Wales and Victoria. Thousands of people from overseas rushed to Australia to make their fortunes. Some became very rich, but others did not make enough money to pay for their journey home. They remained in Australia, swelling the non-Indigenous population from 400,000 in 1850 to 1,100,000 in 1860.

During the 1850s, most of the Australian colonies had been granted self-government. But by the 1890s a growing number of Australians had begun to think that the separate colonies would fare better as a single nation. Among other things, this would mean that Britain would no longer be able to tax goods crossing Australia's internal borders. In 1897 and 1898, a constitution was drawn up and, on 1 January 1901, the colonies finally became united as a federation of states known as the Commonwealth of Australia.

Focus on: Expedition to the interior

The first European settlers to explore the Australian interior became great celebrities. In 1860, Robert Burke and William Wills led an expedition to cross Australia from south to north. They set out with a two-year supply of food. Burke, Wills and two other men named John King and Charles Gray reached Australia's north coast in 1861, but only one man would survive the return journey. Gray died on the way back. Burke, Wills and King reached one of their old camps and waited there for supplies. The two leaders starved to death. The sole survivor was King, who was rescued by Indigenous Australians.

▼ An illustration of the Burke and Wills expedition setting out from Melbourne on 20 August 1860.

TWENTIETH-CENTURY AUSTRALIA

By 1901, Australia had become a single nation. Nevertheless, it kept close ties with Britain, and the British monarch remained as Australia's head of state. Australia supported Britain in wars and conflicts, and Australian armed forces were involved in fighting in the Boer War (1899-1902) in South Africa. More than 400,000 Australian troops also served on the British side in the First World War (1914-18) in Europe.

THE 'WHITE AUSTRALIA' POLICY

Soon after becoming a federation, Australia passed the Immigration Restriction Bill. This was the start of what became known unofficially as the 'White Australia' policy, which aimed to prevent immigration by non-white, non-European people. For many decades afterwards, most new Australians came from Europe. Some of the key immigration restrictions were not abolished until 1958 and racially based immigration practices lasted until 1973. While discouraging non-white immigration, Australia was trying to attract immigrants from Europe. British people, for example, were encouraged to embark on a 'New Life Down Under' ('down under' meaning the other side of the world) by cheap travel and relocation costs. After the Second World War, immigration increased Australia's population significantly and helped to create a period of increasing wealth.

During the Second World War, Robert Menzies was prime minister of Australia. He held office again between 1949 and 1966, and oversaw a period of prosperity for many people. Menzies kept close ties with Britain and is Australia's longest-serving prime minister.

▼ A photographer records the landing of Australian troops on the south-east coast of Borneo in 1945.

WARS ABROAD

During the First World War, young Australian men went to Europe to fight for Britain. Many of these 'Diggers', as they are called, lost their lives at battles such as Gallipoli, where almost 8,000 Australian soldiers died and nearly 20,000 were wounded. During the Second World War (1939-45) many Australian soldiers went to Europe and North Africa to fight. They returned home to defend Australia and fight the Japanese after Japan entered the war in 1941. This 'War in the Pacific' created close links with the USA, which proved to be a more useful ally than far-distant Britain. Australia's involvement in conflict in Asia continued with US-led wars against communist forces in Korea (1950-53) and Vietnam (1957-75).

In 1964, conscription was introduced, and many young Australian men were sent to fight in Vietnam. The Vietnam War and the conscription that accompanied it were a turning point for Australia. Many Australians objected to young men being sent to fight in a war they did not support, and protests followed.

A CHANGE OF GOVERNMENT

Public disapproval of Australia's involvement in the Vietnam War contributed towards the election of a new government in 1972. The new prime minister, Gough Whitlam, made far-reaching changes. His government withdrew troops from Vietnam, abolished conscription, introduced free national healthcare, and supported Indigenous Australians in their attempts to regain some of the land they had once occupied. However, he also presided over a period of high unemployment and inflation.

▶ In Sydney, demonstrators protest against the Vietnam War in 1966.

In 1975, Whitlam was sacked as prime minister by the governor general, the unelected representative of the British crown in Australia. This action sowed the seeds of a debate that continues today: should Australia free itself of its ties with the UK and become a republic, or should it remain a constitutional monarchy?

During the 1980s, Australia became more open to immigration from Asia. Some of the new immigrants were people from Korea and Vietnam, whose parents' generation had seen Australian troops fighting in their countries.

CHAPTER 3

Landscape and Climate

▲ Salt lakes such as this one, which is relatively small, form in Australia's driest inland regions.

Australia is one of the oldest landmasses on earth. Parts of its western area, called the Australian Craton, are 3.8 billion (3,800 million) years old. Its eastern area, the Tasman Fold Belt, is far younger, at 250-500 million years old. The whole continent is slowly drifting northwards, at just 55 mm (2.25 in) a year.

Lying beneath about 20 per cent of Australia is one of the world's largest groundwater stores, the Great Artesian Basin. The Outback of eastern Australia depends on the Basin for its water supplies.

HILLS, DESERTS AND SALT LAKES

Australia's east coast has a narrow, fertile strip of land at the Pacific Ocean's edge. Behind this, the land rises up into the Great Dividing

Range, a line of hills that stretches from north to south across almost the whole continent. The Great Dividing Range is not particularly high in most places – even Mount Kosciuszko, Australia's highest mountain, is just 2,229 m (7,313 ft), less than half the height of Mont Blanc in France and just over a third as high as Mount McKinley in the USA.

West of the Great Dividing Range, the landscape becomes the increasingly flat and dry Outback. This interior landscape is mainly one of barren semi-deserts and dry salt lakes, with some areas able to support sheep and other livestock farms. The flatness of the landscape is broken only by rock outcrops such as Uluru and Kata Tjuta (the Olgas). There are also a few mountainous areas, such as the MacDonnell Ranges near Alice Springs in the centre of Australia.

Western Australia is made up mainly of a broad plateau. The southern strip of the west coast has a fertile area beside the Indian Ocean, but further north the Outback extends as far as the sea.

Australia divides into four basic climate zones: tropical, mostly in northern areas; desert, mostly in the Outback; semi-tropical, mainly in south-eastern areas; and temperate, mainly in the south.

 Did you know?

Some Australian rocks contain crystals dating from 3.8 billion years ago. They are so old that they were once part of the earth's original crust.

Focus on: Uluru and Kata Tjuta

Uluru is a rock formation that soars up out of the flat desert lands in the Australian Outback. It is 3.6 km (2.2 miles) long and 348 m (1,142 ft) high. About two-thirds of the rock is hidden beneath the sandy soil that makes up the surrounding land. Uluru attracts many visitors, keen to see the way the rock changes colour at different times of day – from deep ochre at sunrise and sunset, to brighter reds as the sun climbs higher in the sky. Thirty kilometres (19 miles) or so west of Uluru is another mysterious rock formation, Kata Tjuta. This is a collection of smaller, rounder rocks, and its name means 'many heads' in the local Aboriginal language.

▶ This famous viewpoint looks out over the edge of the Blue Mountains escarpment (steep cliff face), and is visited by thousands of people each month.

RAINFALL AND DROUGHT

Northern Australia is sometimes called the 'Top End', and has a climate distinct from the rest of the country. This region is tropical, with most of its rainfall concentrated into a short season. Parts of the north-east coast of Queensland can receive as much as 380 cm (150 in) of rain a year, compared with the 25-50 cm (10-20 in) received by most of the rest of the country. This is where Australia's remaining areas of rainforest are located.

The Top End has just two seasons: a wet one, from November to April, and a dry one. The wet season can bring violent storms, known as cyclones. In 1974, the coastal town of Darwin was almost flattened by a cyclone.

A less extreme wet season brings rainfall to the south-east and far south-west coasts. The non-wet season of these regions can be very dry, and even areas with reasonable annual rainfall often experience drought. One difficulty caused by drought is forest fire. The fires happen during the dry season, when the vegetation has lost its moisture and easily catches light. Forest fires have always been a part of Australia's ecosystem, and most trees and plants have adapted to survive them, for example, by developing fire-resistant seeds. However, in recent years increasing numbers of people have built homes in the scrubby forested areas, or 'bush', in the coastal hinterlands and on high ground. These homes can easily be destroyed if a fire springs up nearby.

The Outback is the driest region of Australia, and many areas here receive less than 25 cm (10 in) of rain each year. The soils are thin and only a few tough plants can grow without irrigation and shade.

TEMPERATURE

The tropical northern region of Australia has warm or hot temperatures all year round. The town of Cairns, for example, has permanent temperatures of 20-30 °C (68-86 °F), which mean that people wear shorts and a T-shirt all year round. The same is not true of the far south: in Tasmania, the city of Hobart's average temperatures range between 5°C and 20 °C (41°F and 68 °F). In winter, the temperature can fall below freezing for several days in a row. The same is true in Melbourne on the mainland. However,

◀ The temperate rainforests of New South Wales and Queensland are a popular attraction. The money visitors spend here helps to conserve these important environments.

many of Australia's coastal cities have temperatures somewhere between these two extremes, with warm weather for much of the year.

The Australian Outback sees the widest variations of temperature. Daytime temperatures regularly exceed 40 °C (104 °F) during the summer, and at night-time the thermometer often drops below freezing. The hottest months are during the Australian summer, from October to March.

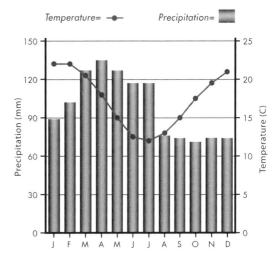

▲ Average monthly climate conditions in Sydney

Did you know?

Australia's southern Alps are covered in snow in winter. They are the only place on the continent where people can go skiing.

▼ A firefighter radios for help as a forest fire blazes out of control in the Australian bush outside Sydney.

Population and Settlements

There are only about 20 million people living in Australia compared with, for example, 290 million living in the USA, even though Australia is more or less the same size as mainland USA (excluding Alaska). This suggests that Australians live surrounded by plenty of open space, and in a sense this is true – there are large, empty spaces all over Australia. But many parts of the country are not suitable for people to live in. The lack of water and other resources, together with the hot, dry climate, mean that large areas of the Outback can only support a small population. Most Australians inhabit cities or towns and live close to other people.

CITIES AND SUBURBS

The city centres of Sydney, Melbourne and Perth, for example, are home to a relatively young population although, of course, older people also live there. Clubs, restaurants, bars and sports venues cater for these city-living Australians. The inner cities are becoming increasingly popular places to live.

 Did you know?

Forecasts predict that by 2030, 96 per cent of Australians will live in cities and towns.

Most Australians, however, live in the suburbs. These are urban areas outside the city centres. Typical homes in the suburbs are bigger than in the city centres, and are often detached houses with large gardens and, sometimes, a swimming pool.

Since 1950, Australia's population has grown, and an increasing number of Australians have started to live in cities. In 1950, 75.1 per cent of

◄ A busy street in Sydney showing (centre top) the rail that carries the monorail train around the city centre.

▲ Suburban houses like these tend to be a long way from shops and other facilities, which is one reason why Australians often use their cars to get around.

Australians lived in an urban environment. By 2005, that figure had reached 92 per cent. As the urban population has grown, so too has the area covered by the suburbs. In Sydney, for example, the western suburbs now stretch out to the Blue Mountains, which form a barrier to further suburban expansion. These suburbs are over an hour's journey from the city centre. Many Australians depend on their cars to travel long distances to work every day from the sprawling suburbs.

RICH AND POOR

Australia's various suburbs are very different in character. Sydney's northern beaches, for example, are home to some of the most glamorous properties in the country, including ultra-modern steel and glass villas overlooking

beautiful stretches of sea and shore. At the other extreme are the suburban areas – often inland and far from the city centre – which have traditionally been home to poorly paid workers and new immigrants.

Population data

- Population: 20.2 million
- Population 0-14 yrs: 20%
- Population 15-64 yrs: 68%
- Population 65+ yrs: 12%
- Population growth rate: 1.1%
- Population density: 2.6 per sq km/6.8 per sq mile
- Urban population: 92%
- Major cities: Sydney 4,388,000, Melbourne 3,663,000, Brisbane 1,769,000, Perth 1,484,000, Adelaide 1,137,000

Source: United Nations and World Bank

NEW IMMIGRANTS

Much of the growth in Australia's population during the twentieth century was the result of immigration. Initially immigrants tended to come from Europe – in 1901, almost 80 per cent of immigrant Australians were from Britain. Later in the century, a smaller proportion of immigrants were from Britain, and by 1954 the figure was just 52 per cent. Also in 1954, 33 per cent of European immigrants were from Italy, Greece, Germany, the Netherlands and Poland.

During the 1980s and 1990s, after the abolition of racially based immigration laws (see page 12), immigrants began to arrive from South-east Asia and the Indian subcontinent. By 2002, 15 per cent of immigrant Australians were from Asian or Pacific countries such as China, Vietnam, the Philippines, India, Malaysia and Sri Lanka. In 1954, people from these countries had made up just 2 per cent of immigrant Australians.

New immigrants typically live in major cities, where they are more likely to find work and come across other people who speak their language and are familiar with their culture. This means that rural areas have not received as many immigrants as Australian towns and cities. As a result, the government now makes it easier for people to immigrate to Australia if they are willing to spend time working in rural areas.

SHRINKING RURAL POPULATIONS

In the main, Australia's rural towns grew up as focal points for the local economy. In agricultural areas, they were places where farmers could bring their goods to market, for transport on to the big cities. Other rural towns grew up around different industries, such as mining.

 Did you know?

The world's largest cattle farm is at Anna Creek, Australia, and covers 34,000 sq km (13,127 sq m), which makes it bigger than the country of Belgium.

◀ The entrance to Sydney's Chinatown district. Increasing numbers of Chinese people have migrated to Australia since the 1980s. Many recent immigrants have also come from elsewhere in Asia.

As long as the mines stay open – and mining is one of Australia's biggest industries – rural mining towns have tended to survive, and even thrive. The same cannot be said of some towns in farming areas. The increase in long-distance travel, the effect of the Internet upon rural businesses (which now have to compete with far-off shops in the cities, and lose customers as a result), and the lure of the facilities in bigger cities have stripped many rural towns of their businesses and young people.

Since 1950, Australia's rural population has shrunk at a rate of up to 4 per cent every five years. In 1950, there were just over 2 million Australians living in rural areas; by 2000, this had dropped to 1.8 million, and it is forecast that this figure will be fewer than 1 million by 2030. At the same time, the overall population has increased, meaning that a smaller and smaller proportion of Australians live in rural areas.

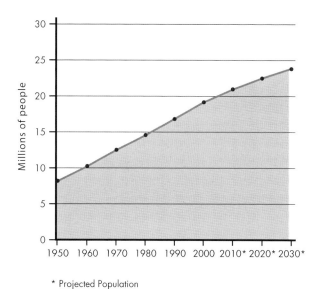

* Projected Population

▲ Population growth, 1950-2030

▼ Greek-Australian dancers perform a traditional Greek dance at a festival in Gosford, New South Wales.

Government and Politics

Australia is a federal state, which means that it has a central government but the different territories have powers to control some of their own affairs. The main political parties are the Australian Labor Party and the Liberal Party. Other smaller parties include the National Country Party and the Australian Democrats.

FEDERAL GOVERNMENT

The federal government controls Australia's economy, taxes, immigration, defence and foreign policy. The government is based in Canberra, which has its own territory, the Australian Capital Territory (ACT). The ACT, which surrounds the city, means that Canberra is independent of the other states, as it is not a part of any of them.

One reason for ACT's existence is the rivalry that exists between Australia's states, especially between Victoria and New South Wales. If Sydney in New South Wales had become the capital city, the people of Victoria would have been unhappy. If Melbourne in Victoria had been chosen, the people of New South Wales would have been disappointed. In the end, a whole new city, Canberra, was built, with a new territory around it.

No government is allowed to remain in office for more than three years without an election being held. Usually the prime minister, the leader of the government, chooses to call an election before the three year term is up.

▼ Tourists view the Australian National Parliament House from the summit of Mount Ainslie in Canberra.

▶ Prime Minister John Howard holds a Bible as his Liberal Party government is sworn-in in Canberra on 26 October 2004.

The government is made up of two parts, the House of Representatives and the Senate. There are 148 members in the House of Representatives. Each of Australia's eight states and territories elects a number of representatives based on its population (which means the states with the biggest populations get the most representatives). The numbers in 2006 were: New South Wales 50 representatives, Victoria 37, Queensland 27, South Australia 12, Western Australia 14, Tasmania 5, ACT 2, and Northern Territory 1. The political party with the most seats in the House of Representatives chooses the ministers who will run the country, including the prime minister.

The second governing body is the Senate. This has 12 senators from each of the six states, and two from each of the territories. The Senate can block legislation from the House of Representatives, balancing power between the large and small states.

 Did you know?

Voting in elections is compulsory in Australia. However, prosecutions for failure to vote are rare and fines are nominal.

Focus on: Canberra

Canberra is one of the few cities in the world that did not grow up from a smaller settlement. Instead in 1912 US architect, Walter Burley Griffin, won an international competition to design it from scratch. Canberra's name was taken from an Aboriginal word thought to mean 'meeting place'. Canberra is halfway between Sydney and Melbourne, and is the only major Australian city not to be on the coast. The Australian parliament first met there in 1927, though the city was not really finished until after the Second World War.

STATE GOVERNMENT

State governments are led by a premier or, in Northern Territory, a chief minister. The difference between the two roles is in name only. The structure of government is usually the same as for the national government, with two governing bodies, although Queensland abolished its upper house in 1922.

The main responsibilities of the state governments are for health, education, housing, transport and local law enforcement. Most taxes are raised by the federal government, which then releases some of this money to the states. The money from the federal government is rarely sufficient for major new works such as, for example, large sports facilities or new roads. Money for these is raised through extra payments or loans, usually from the federal government. This means that there is a lot of federal control over the state governments.

LOCAL GOVERNMENT

Within each state there is a third layer of government, made up mainly of shire (shires are small rural regions), town or city councils. These maintain and build local roads, make sure rubbish is collected, fund local libraries and perform other similar day-to-day tasks. Local government, like state government, is mainly financed from federal funds.

▼ Queen Elizabeth II of Britain plants a gum tree in the grounds of Government House in Canberra during the course of a five-day official visit to Australia in March 2006. She is watched by gardener Norm Dunn (left) and Prince Philip (right).

Focus on: Republicanism

Australia has the British monarch as head of state. For many years, some Australians have wanted their country to become a republic and cut its ties with the British monarchy. This idea dates back hundreds of years. Irish people were among Australia's earliest settlers and they arrived in the country with no love of the British monarchy. The republican debate came to a head during the early 1990s, when Paul Keating was prime minister of Australia. Keating was a republican who thought Australia should sever its ties with the 'old country' – a term that was increasingly irrelevant to immigrant Australians who had no ties to Britain. In 1999, Australia held a referendum to decide whether or not to become a republic. Almost every state rejected the proposal to become a republic, and Australia kept its ties with Britain.

CITIES AND STATES

In some big cities, local government is divided between several areas of the city. This prevents the cities from becoming too powerful within the state. Sydney, for example, has 39 separate local government regions. This is partly because most of the people in New South Wales live within the area of Greater Sydney. If these people were to elect their own mayor (which they do not at the moment), the result could be that more people voted for the mayor of Sydney than supported the premier of New South Wales. In this case, the mayor of Sydney would be in a potentially powerful position, even though he or she ranked below the state premier.

 Did you know?

In the national referendum of 1999, only the Australian Capital Territory voted 'yes' to the idea of a republic.

▶ The exterior of the New South Wales state parliament building in Sydney.

CHAPTER 6

Energy and Resources

Most of Australia's energy – 91.6 per cent of its electricity, for example – comes from fossil fuels (oil, coal and natural gas). Of the rest, the bulk comes from hydro-electric power, which provides 7.2 per cent of Australia's electricity. Australia is the world's fourth biggest producer and its biggest exporter of coal. It also has large natural gas reserves, and produces 8 per cent of the world's supplies. Natural gas production in Australia is projected to more than double between 1980 and 2020.

Australia does not have access to large amounts of its own oil, although there are reserves off the coast of Victoria and in South and Western Australia. Australia's known commercial oil reserves will probably be used up by 2015, compared with 2065 for natural gas and 2105 for coal. Of course, more energy resources may be found, and geologists have identified offshore regions where such discoveries may be made. Even so, oil now has to be imported,

which places a drain on Australia's economy as the country has to buy expensive oil from abroad instead of providing its own.

ENERGY CONSUMPTION

Australians use a lot of energy, even compared with people in other wealthy nations. In 2000, each Australian used the equivalent of 5.8 tonnes of oil compared with Japan's 4.1, the UK's 3.9, Mexico's 1.6 or Vietnam's 0.5 tonnes. (Higher users of energy include Canada at 8.2 tonnes per person, the USA at 8.4 tonnes, and Kuwait at 10.5 tonnes.)

There are various reasons for Australia's high energy use. The first is Australians' dependency on their cars. This is linked to the size of the country where, outside the city centres, walking or cycling is not always practical. Also, some big Australian industries, such as mining, metal production and ore extraction, are typically large consumers of energy. A further reason is

◀ This terrifying looking machine doesn't come from the set of a *Mad Max* movie – it is a cutting machine for an open-cast coal mine.

Australia's hot climate, which makes energy hungry appliances like air conditioning units common in some areas and increases the energy demands made by its citizens.

ALTERNATIVE ENERGIES

Apart from hydro-electric power, Australia gets little of its energy from alternative sources. Given the country's long hours of sunshine, solar power offers abundant opportunities for this to change in the future. The Australian government is committed to trying to increase the use of alternative energies, through hydro-electric, solar, biomass and wind power.

NUCLEAR POWER

Although Australia is a major exporter of nuclear-power-grade uranium, it does not produce any of its own energy using nuclear power stations. The country's supplies of cheap coal have in the past made nuclear power unnecessary.

▲ Parabolic solar energy dishes at a power station operated by the Solar Research Corporation of Melbourne.

? Did you know?

Skiing became popular in Australia after 1949, when European hydro-electric workers on the Snowy Mountains power scheme practised the sport. It is now a favourite winter pastime.

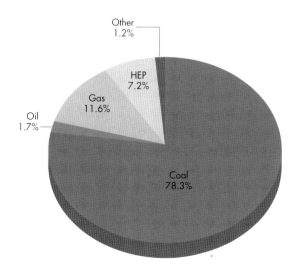

▲ Electricity production by type

Other 1.2%
HEP 7.2%
Gas 11.6%
Oil 1.7%
Coal 78.3%

Energy data

▷ Energy consumption as % of world total: 1.1%

▷ Energy consumption by sector (% of total)

Industry:	34.6
Transportation:	39.2
Agriculture:	2.3
Services:	7.0
Residential:	12.6
Other:	4.3

▷ CO_2 emissions as % of world total: 1.4

▷ CO_2 emissions per capita in tonnes p.a.: 17.4

Source: World Resources Institute

▲ A miner in the opal fields near Lightning Ridge, New South Wales.

MINERAL RESOURCES

Australia is rich in mineral resources. First to be discovered were reserves of copper, gold, silver, lead, tin and zinc during the 1800s. Deposits of diamonds were also found, as were the world's biggest deposits of high quality opals. Then, during the 1950s, geologists found huge deposits of iron ore, coal and bauxite (needed for the manufacture of aluminium).

Western Australia, Queensland and New South Wales are the top three mining states. Western Australia has large reserves of nickel, iron ore, gold and bauxite. Copper, silver and bauxite are found in Queensland and coal, lead and zinc are found in New South Wales. Australia is thought to have the world's largest undeveloped deposits of uranium, in the Northern Territory and South Australia.

These mineral resources are often found in the least hospitable parts of the country, which means that the people who work them often live in isolated settlements. Roads and railways need to be built to reach new mines, making it expensive to develop new mining areas. Even so, Australia is one of the world's leading miners of mineral resources.

AGRICULTURAL RESOURCES

Although a third of Australia is desert landscape, there are large coastal areas where the soil is suitable for farming. While farmland covers about 60 per cent of the country, only 10 per cent of it is suitable for crop growing. The rest is used as pastureland for animals, mainly sheep and cattle.

In the north, specialist crops – tropical fruits such as mangoes, and flowers such as orchids – can be grown. Heading further south, crops more associated with temperate climates become common. Here are found fruits such as

Focus on: Coober Pedy

The town of Coober Pedy in South Australia advertises itself as 'The Opal Capital of the World'. It grew up around a cluster of opal mines, and its name is said to be a version of the Indigenous Australian words 'kupa piti', meaning 'white man in a hole'. Today, the town still supplies almost all the world's high-grade opal gemstones, but it has also become an unlikely tourist attraction. People come to visit the mines and see the unique underground lifestyle of the town. In the past, the baking desert heat drove some of the townspeople to live underground, where their homes (called 'dugouts' by locals) stayed cool during the heat of the day.

apples, together with sugar, wheat, potatoes, rice, and grapes for winemaking.

Australia's fishing resources are limited. There are thousands of different kinds of fish in the waters off Australia, but few edible ones are present in large numbers. Australia's biggest fishing resource is shellfish, including abalone, lobster, oyster, shrimp and scallop.

The cooler southern regions of Australia have large forested areas where commercial quantities of wood can be harvested. Tasmania, in particular, has large areas of old-growth forest, which provide a major natural resource. Tasmania's trees include the unique and rare huon pines, said to be the best wood for boat-building. However, logging these forests is highly controversial because it has generally not been carried out in a sustainable way. Opponents claim that the logging industry is doing irreparable harm to the environment and animals, including many endangered species.

 Did you know?

Australia produces nearly all its own food.

▼ Workers picking grapes at a vineyard in the Hunter Valley, east of Sydney. Wine is a relatively recent export crop for Australia, but it is now a highly valuable one.

CHAPTER 7

Economy and Income

Australia is a wealthy country, with a GNI per person slightly higher than that of Hong Kong, Italy and Spain. By any measure, Australians enjoy a good standard of living. In 2004-5, Australia was ranked twenty-fourth in the world by per person GNI.

MINING AND AGRICULTURE

Australia's natural and mineral resources are important to its economy. Australia's wealth was built on the twin foundations of agriculture and mining, and these remain a vital part of today's economy. They are particularly important for exports: the products of agriculture and mining together make up roughly 65 per cent of all Australia's exported goods.

Mining and agriculture (including fishing and forestry) each contribute similar amounts to the Australian economy – mining contributes 4.9 per cent and agriculture contributes 3 per cent. They also support the manufacturing industries, such as metal production or food and animal processing. For example, the iron ore mines produce ore but also supply Australia's important metal-processing industry. The manufacturing industries contribute a further 15 per cent to the economy.

Mining and agriculture also contribute towards the wholesale and retail trades, where finished goods such as sheet metal or meat and vegetables are sold. While many of these goods are produced outside Australia, a proportion of the 10 per cent contribution to the economy of this sector is derived from goods that are produced within Australia.

▼ A fisherman unloads and sorts the sardine catch at the wharf in Lakes Entrance, Victoria.

Many agricultural businesses are founded upon animal husbandry, particularly cattle and sheep farming. Live animals and processed meat are produced for the home market and exported, and animal products such as wool also provide income. Grain is produced for the home market and is another important export crop.

Australia's valuable mineral exports include metals, coal and natural gas. Most of the country's mineral resources, such as its vast uranium deposits, remain untapped. This means that mining is set to play an important part in the Australian economy in the future.

FOREIGN OWNERSHIP

In the past, Australia lacked capital – money to invest in developing new industrial sites -– and this made it difficult to develop its economy. It meant that many businesses had to borrow capital from abroad. As a result, many mining companies, factories, processing plants and other businesses are foreign owned, by companies from the UK, USA, Japan or elsewhere. The Australian government recently passed a law declaring that at least 50 per cent

of new mining projects had to be Australian owned, but even today lack of capital means that this requirement is not always enforced.

▼ At the port of Adelaide, sheep are loaded on to a ship for export to the Middle East. Many animal rights activists say this export of live animals is cruel.

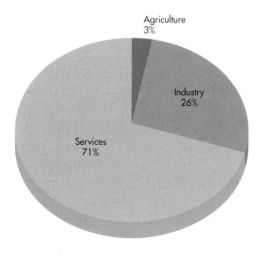

▲ Contribution by sector to national income

Economic data

- Gross National Income (GNI) in US$: 541,173,481,472
- World rank by GNI: 14
- GNI per capita in US$: 26,900
- World rank by GNI per capita: 24
- Economic growth: 3.0%

Source: World Bank

SERVICE INDUSTRIES

Although Australia's wealth traditionally came from mining and agriculture, the economy is now dominated by service industries. Taken together, in 2005, service industries contributed 71 per cent (an increase of 9 per cent on the 2002 figure) of total GDP.

Service industries include banking, financial and property services (the largest sector), which contribute 17.5 per cent of GDP. Other important service industries include retail and wholesale trade (10.2 per cent of GDP); transport and communications (7.7 per cent), and construction (6.3 per cent).

▼ The Macquarie Bank in Sydney – founded in 1970 with 3 members of staff, the bank is now one of Australia's most important financial organizations.

The fastest growth in the service sector has been in communications including, for example, the provision of telephone and email services. The communications industry has recently averaged a growth rate of 6.4 per cent. The most precarious sector is construction. During the 1990s and early 2000s, Australia experienced a boom in the cost of housing, especially in the big cities, and this has fuelled growth in the construction industry. However, the boom in house prices has ended and the people working in construction are now vulnerable to the threat of unemployment.

TOURISM

Tourism, which was substantially boosted when Sydney hosted the 2000 Olympic Games, makes

an important contribution to Australia's economy. Tourists spend substantial amounts of money in a variety of service industries, including travel, retail, accommodation and the restaurant trade.

Almost half the total of tourist dollars is spent outside the major cities, so tourism is important to rural as well as urban economies. In 2003-4, over half a million Australians worked in the tourist industry, which brought Aus$7.6 billion to the country's coffers. Total spending by international visitors was Aus$17.3 billion.

Did you know?

Australian women earn almost one-third less than Australian men.

▲ Tourists watch the sun setting on Uluru. The site is a major Australian landmark, attracting around 400,000 visitors every year.

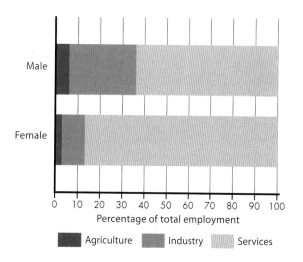

▲ Labour force by sector and gender

Global Connections

In the past, Australia's main foreign links were with the West, especially the UK and later the USA. Even after Australia was united as a federation in 1901, it retained very close links with the UK, and tended to follow its lead in matters of foreign policy, as shown by the decision to join the fight in Europe during the First World War. The families of many Australians had originally come from the UK, and Australia still believed and trusted in its strong connection with the 'old country'. When Britain declared war on Germany in 1939, the Australian Prime Minister Robert Menzies said: 'There can be no doubt that where Great Britain stands, there stand the people of the entire British world.' As a result, Australia too joined the Second World War in 1939.

During the conflict, Australia was threatened with the possibility of an invasion by forces from Japan (then an ally of Germany). Between 1942 and 1943, Japanese aircraft bombed northern Australian targets a total of 93 times and killed hundreds of people. By this point, Britain's almost singlehanded involvement in the war in Europe since 1939 had left it in a weakened state, and it was unable or unwilling to send help. Australia found instead that it had common interests with the USA, which was also fighting Japanese forces in the Pacific region. The two countries worked together closely. By 1942, the US Army's Pacific headquarters were based in Australia and more than 120,000 US troops were stationed there.

THE COLD WAR

As the twentieth century progressed, Australia's links with the USA became more important. Australia was a strong ally of the USA in its Cold War attempts to defeat communism in Asia. During the 1950s, Australia joined two international organizations led by the USA. ANZUS linked Australia, New Zealand and

◀ Two young British women on board a ship carrying emigrants to Australia in the 1940s.

▲ The USA's influence is felt in Australia in the form of an old 1950s-style American car, being used here during a wedding in the 'Rocks' area of Sydney.

the USA, while SEATO linked the ANZUS countries plus the UK and France with Thailand, Pakistan, Cambodia, South Vietnam and Laos, in an anti-communist alliance.

Between 1950 and the 1970s, Australia sent troops to help US forces in wars in Korea and Vietnam. The Vietnam War became highly unpopular with many Australians, who wanted to know why their young men needed to be sent to fight in a country with which they had no particular quarrel. Australia's warm relationship with the USA cooled when Australian troops were brought home from the Vietnam War in 1972. The USA's own involvement in Vietnam did not end until 1975.

The Australian government's support for US-led invasions of Afghanistan in 2001 and Iraq in 2003 cemented friendly relations with the USA once more. Possibly as a result of this, Australia agreed a free-trade agreement with the USA in 2005.

UN INVOLVEMENT

Australia is strongly involved in United Nations (UN) activities, including human rights work, economic development, weapons control, the fight against the trade in illegal drugs, and peacekeeping. In September 1999, Australia led an international UN peacekeeping force in East Timor. In 1975, Indonesian forces had occupied East Timor, and the local people had accused them of many human rights abuses. In 1999, East Timor voted to become independent, but in

 Did you know?

About 29,000 Australians died in action during the Second World War.

an act of revenge Indonesian militias began attacking the East Timorese people. Australia led the UN force that restored order and helped the country to become independent in May 2002.

REGIONAL ORGANIZATIONS

Australia has recently played a peacekeeping role in Papua New Guinea and the Solomon Islands. These countries are fellow members of the Pacific Islands Forum, an organization that connects countries in the Pacific region. Members of the forum co-operate in efforts to maintain security, improve living standards and ensure sustainable development in the region.

Australia works to develop close links with many of its Asian neighbours, and is part of the Association of South-east Asian Nations Regional Forum. Australia gives over a billion US dollars in aid to poorer countries, and much of this is given in Asia. For example, Papua New Guinea, Thailand and Indonesia all received substantial aid packages in the 1990s, and Australia provided immediate help to the Asian countries affected by the huge *tsunami* of December 2004.

Australia's links in the Asian Pacific also help in its trading relations with countries such as Japan and China, among others.

THE COMMONWEALTH

In addition to regional links, Australia is an active member of the Commonwealth, a group of countries that were once governed by Britain. The Commonwealth connects wealthy countries, such as Australia and the UK, with poorer countries, to try to help cultural understanding and economic development. It also organizes the Commonwealth Games, which Australia has hosted four times, most recently in 2006 in Melbourne, Victoria.

The Commonwealth is less important for trade than was once the case, but Australia still retains trade links with many Commonwealth countries.

 Did you know?

Australia was one of the countries that helped draft the United Nations Charter, which was signed in 1945.

◀ Peacekeeping troops, with an Australian soldier in the foreground, carry out a security patrol of Dili's airport at the beginning of UN 'Operation Stabilize' in East Timor in 1999.

Focus on: Terrorism and the Muslim world

During the late 1990s and into the twenty-first century, Australia became increasingly unpopular in the Muslim world. One reason for this was that it had supported two US-led invasions of Muslim countries (Afghanistan in 2001 and Iraq in 2003).

Another reason was that it had given support to East Timor, whose mainly Catholic population had demanded independence from Indonesian (mainly Muslim) control. In October 2002, a terrorist bomb attack on the island of Bali in Indonesia killed 202 people. Bali is a favourite holiday resort for Australians, and they numbered 89 of the dead. Muslim terrorists claimed responsibility for the Bali bombing. In 2005, a second bomb attack in Bali killed a further 23 people, including four Australians.

Australia's generous aid to victims of the 2004 *tsunami* disaster resulted in an increase in its popularity in Asian Muslim countries once more. At the same time, Australia toughened up its immigration policies, in the hope of keeping Muslim extremists out of the country.

◀ A memorial to the Bali bombing victims stands at Coogee Beach in Sydney.

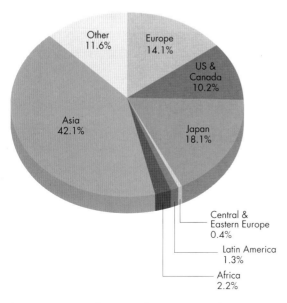

▲ Destination of exports by major trading region

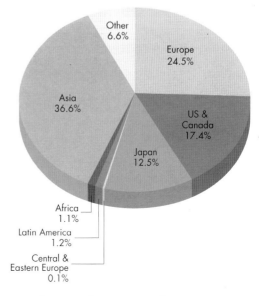

▲ Origin of imports by major trading region

CHAPTER 9

Transport and Communications

Australia's huge size and the inhospitable climate of its interior have always made it uncomfortable and sometimes dangerous to travel long distances within the country. The first European settlers to arrive in Australia took many years to break out of Sydney and through the 'barrier' of the Blue Mountains (see page 19). All Australia's first settlements were on good anchorages, because it was far easier to move from place to place by sea than overland.

Even today, there are sometimes large and inhospitable areas between settlements. People planning to drive in the interior of some areas of Western Australia, for example, are warned to carry extra water and food with them because, if their car breaks down, they may have a long wait before help arrives. Australian transport routes tend to link together the main settlements. Exceptions include roads or railways that have been built to reach industrial sites, such as mines.

Transport & communications data

- Total roads: 811,603 km/504,321 miles
- Total paved roads: 314,090 km/ 195,172 miles
- Total unpaved roads: 497,513 km/ 309,149 miles
- Total railways: 54,439 km/33,828 miles
- Airports: 450
- Cars per 1,000 people: 635
- Mobile phones per 1,000 people: 719.5
- Personal computers per 1,000 people: 565.1
- Internet users per 1,000 people: 566.7

Source: World Bank and CIA World Factbook

WATER TRANSPORT

Water transport remains an important link between Australia's coastal cities. Ships carry large amounts of minerals along the coasts, and

◄ Giant cranes load and unload containers from ships at Melbourne's international port.

▶ A double-decker train pulls into Summer Hill suburban station, ready to ferry commuters to work in Sydney.

most of Australia's overseas exports are sent by sea. In the east, Gladstone, Hay Point, Melbourne, Newcastle and Sydney are among the busiest ports, though the use of Sydney Harbour as a port has been under debate partly because of fears that it could be a terrorist target. In the west, the busiest ports include Dampier, Fremantle, Port Hedland and Port Walcott.

RAIL TRANSPORT

Main rail lines connect many of Australia's major cities and towns, particularly in the east. Trains mostly carry freight, but many also take passengers. Sydney and Melbourne have extensive networks of local train lines, which provide a fast and inexpensive way to move around the city.

All Australia's main railway lines are government owned. There are also a small number of privately owned railways. These usually belong to mining companies, and are used to transport minerals from the mines to a main railway line.

 Did you know?

The Trans-Australian Railway has the longest stretch of dead straight track in the world.

Focus on: The Trans-Australian Railway

The Trans-Australian Railway is the longest rail line in Australia, stretching 1,783 km (1,108 miles) from Port Pirie in South Australia to Kalgoorlie in Western Australia. Work began at each end of the line in 1913 and the two sections finally met on 17 October 1917. Today, the journey takes 37 hours, and passes through some of Australia's most distinctive landscapes.

Heading east from Kalgoorlie, the train crosses a plateau that is mostly forested with eucalyptus trees. Next it reaches a treeless area where only low bushes grow. Part of this is the Nullarbor Plain, where the line runs straight for 497 km (309 miles). Finally, the train heads across the red soil and low hills of South Australia towards Port Pirie.

AIR TRAVEL

Australia has an extensive network of airports. The main cities each have international airports, and there are also smaller terminals for flights within Australia. In Outback areas, a large sheep station may also have its own small aircraft and a landing strip for small planes. Some farmers even use helicopters in animal herding.

ROAD TRANSPORT

Most Australian families own at least one car, which is their main way of getting around. The cities have excellent road networks, although with so much car use they can become very crowded at busy times of the day, especially when people are travelling to and from work. Long traffic jams are common, and it can be as quick to walk as to drive short distances through the city centres.

Major towns and cities are connected by a good series of mainly two-lane roads. Minor roads outside built-up areas are often unpaved, as are many of the roads in the Outback. Instead, people drive along levelled dirt tracks.

Cycling any distance in the heat of the Outback is not very practical. But many Australian cities are keen to increase cycle use because cycling is healthy and does not cause pollution or congestion. There are problems, however, as few streets are designed for the purpose, and Australian drivers are not particularly aware of the safety of cyclists. The introduction of cycle routes will encourage more people to get on their bikes, and an increasing number of routes are being completed each year.

MODERN COMMUNICATIONS

Almost one in three Australians buys a newspaper every day, compared with, for example, one in five Americans. As a result, Australians are generally well informed. They also receive regular news updates on TV.

The numbers of telephone lines (one for every two people in 2001), personal computer owners

▼ The domestic departure terminal at Sydney airport. Low-cost airlines have made travelling around Australia cheaper and faster than ever before.

and Internet users (more than one in every two people too) have all grown rapidly, and continue to do so. Modern communications systems such as telephones, mobile phones and email have revolutionized life for many Australians, especially those in the Outback or other remote areas. Previously, buying non-local goods might have involved a long journey. Today it is possible to browse a website or catalogue, pick up the phone and order whatever you want. Medical advice and education are also available via the Internet and email, and people in isolated communities can make contact with others who have similar interests, even if they live thousands of kilometres apart.

 Did you know?

Australia had 142 airports with unpaved runways in 2005.

▲ An opal miner uses a solar powered phone in a Queensland Outback town. Modern telecommunications such as this are extremely important in the more remote areas of Australia.

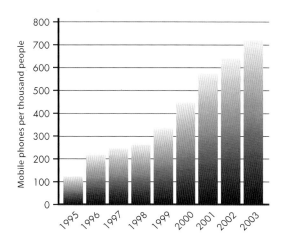

▲ Mobile phone use, 1995-2003

Education and Health

Each Australian state or territory runs its own education system, paid for with federal funds. The education system therefore varies slightly in different states and territories, for example, with varying amounts of time spent at primary or secondary school. Everywhere, education is divided between primary, secondary and post-secondary levels. All schools across Australia must follow national curriculum guidelines.

STANDARDS OF LITERACY

Australia generally has a good standard of education, with high literacy rates. However, one in five adults lacks some reading and writing skills, and as a result finds it difficult to participate in everyday life. Indigenous Australians have a poor record of educational achievement, and in the past have found it difficult to do well at school. The experience of many Indigenous Australians was that school was an unwelcoming place, where the language, clothing and behaviour were completely different from what they were used to. Even today,

over 10 per cent do not attend, and those who do generally reach lower than average standards of reading by their third year of school. This problem is particularly acute in the Northern Territory, where only about 25 per cent of Indigenous Australian children reached the target standard, against 65 per cent of other students.

STATE AND PRIVATE SCHOOLS

In state-owned and run schools, education is said to be free, though many schools do charge parents a small amount for sending their children there. Private schools, many of them owned and run by the Roman Catholic Church, charge

? Did you know?

The King's School in Sydney is the oldest independent school in Australia. It was founded in 1831.

▼ A typical classroom scene in an Australian primary school.

significantly higher fees for attendance. Private schools have become increasingly popular, because they are thought by some people to offer a better education. Students at both state and private schools usually have to wear uniform, although this is not always the case. Private schools tend to have stricter dress codes.

Many children begin their education at about three years old, when they go to kindergarten or 'pre-primary'. All children must start school by six years of age, which is when they begin primary school. They stay in primary for between six and eight years, then progress to secondary – which is generally called high school – for five or six years. The minimum school-leaving age varies between 15 and 16.

After high school, students can go on to post-secondary education. One option is a one- or two-year vocational training course at an institute of technical and further education, studying a trade such as car mechanics or agricultural science. Other students choose a three- or four-year degree course at a university, studying anything from English literature to chemistry. Graduates of post-secondary education find it easier to obtain work than those who leave school at age 16.

LONG-DISTANCE LEARNING

Many Australian children living in Outback areas are too far from schools to be able to attend. Instead they take their lessons by correspondence course. In the past, these courses were undertaken by post, but the Internet tends to be used today. Every state and territory has a correspondence school for children in isolated locations. Three states and the Northern Territory also have 'schools of the air', where children can contact their teachers directly by radio, fax or computer.

▲ Students outside the university buildings at Sydney.

Education and health

- Life expectancy at birth, male: 76.9
- Life expectancy at birth, female: 82.7
- Infant mortality rate per 1,000: 6
- Under five mortality rate per 1,000: 6
- Physicians per 1,000 people: 2.5
- Health expenditure as % of GDP: 9.5%
- Education expenditure as % of GDP: 4.9%
- Primary net enrolment: 96%
- Pupil-teacher ratio, primary: n/a
- Adult literacy as % age 15+: 99%

Source: United Nations Agencies and World Bank

◀ Today doctors can give advice to patients in far-flung areas of Australia using the Internet.

HEALTHCARE

Healthcare is provided by each of Australia's states and territories, using money that comes mainly from the federal government. National healthcare policies are decided at a federal level. All residents of Australia are entitled to free healthcare at public hospitals, under a scheme called Medicare. Medicare also pays for 85 per cent of the cost of going to see a general practitioner. Medicare is paid for mainly by a 1.5 per cent tax on people's incomes.

People can also choose to be treated privately, either by paying for their treatment direct or through private medical insurance. The latter involves paying a monthly amount to an insurance company which, in return, will pay your future medical costs when you are ill. As in almost every country, the wealthy tend to get higher quality medical treatment and receive it more quickly than do the poor.

NATIONAL AND LOCAL FUNCTIONS

The federal government gives money to public hospitals, residential care facilities and home and community care. It also pays for most of the country's health research and supports the training of health professionals. State and territory governments provide the actual health services, including most hospitals. The states and territories also run a range of community and public health services, including health services in schools, dentists, care for mothers and children, such as pre- and ante-natal classes, and disease control. Local government is mostly involved in environmental health control, such as rubbish disposal, clean water and some health inspections.

STRAINS ON THE SYSTEM

Almost 10 per cent of Australia's GDP is spent on healthcare. This money is being stretched further each year, mainly as a result of demands by Australia's ageing population. People are living longer, so there are more old people still alive. As people get older, they need more help from the health services. At the same time, Australians generally are having fewer children than they did 30 years ago, so in the future there will be fewer taxpayers to contribute to Medicare. Dealing with this issue is likely to present governments with a significant challenge in the future.

Did you know?

Before the Flying Doctors (see box), medical help in the Outback was usually provided by 'Boundary Riders' – who often arrived by camel.

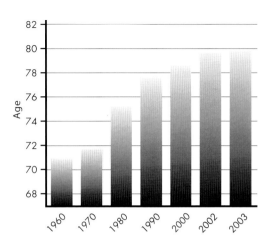

▲ Life expectancy at birth, 1960-2003

Focus on: The Flying Doctors

The Flying Doctors – or, to give it its proper name, the Royal Flying Doctor Service – provide healthcare services to people in remote communities. Founded in 1928 by the Reverend John Flynn, the Flying Doctors treat roughly 183,000 people a year. They have 17 bases, 38 aircraft, and fly over 7,150,000 sq km (2,761,000 sq miles) of territory. In addition to flying into remote areas, the Flying Doctors provide medical advice by radio and telephone.

The Flying Doctors cost roughly Aus$43 million each year and are paid for mainly by grants from the federal, state and territory governments. Donations from business and the general public also help to keep the service going.

◀ A member of the Flying Doctor service transfers a patient from a light aircraft to a waiting ambulance.

CHAPTER 11

Culture and Religion

Australia's original culture is that of the Indigenous Australians, but they are now largely marginalized from society. Very little traditional Indigenous Australian culture and religion spilled into the lives of settler or immigrant Australians.

Since the 1960s, however, Indigenous Australian art has become increasingly sought after in Australia and around the world. The close relationship to the land that is a key part of Indigenous Australian beliefs inspires some of Australia's environmental campaigners, and has influenced some filmmakers, such as Nicolas Roeg (*Walkabout*) and Phillip Noyce (*Rabbit-Proof Fence*). Indigenous Australian actors such as Ernie Dingo and musicians like Yothu Yindi have also been successful.

RELIGION

Australia's constitution forbids state religion and guarantees people freedom of worship. Most Australians are Christian, usually either Protestant or Roman Catholic, but few people attend church regularly. The Uniting Church, which was formed by Methodists, Congregationalists and Presbyterians in 1977, is the third-largest Christian church. There are

▼ Les Saxby, an Indigenous Australian musician, plays a traditional instrument known as a *didgeridoo*. He is playing on the shore of Botany Bay, at the exact spot where Captain Cook's expedition first landed in Australia in 1788. Each year, the 'Meeting of Two Cultures' ceremony takes place here, attended by local community groups to mark the subsequent events.

also small Jewish and Muslim communities in the cities. Over 16 per cent of Australians are atheist or claim no religion at all.

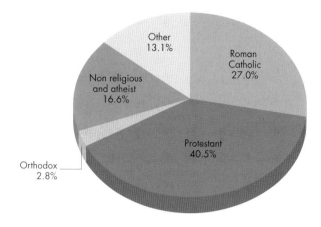

▲ Major religions

LITERATURE

Australia is home to some of the great writers of the twentieth and twenty-first centuries. The novelist Patrick White, for example, won the Nobel Prize for Literature in 1973. Another author, Thomas Keneally, wrote the novel *Schindler's List*, on which Steven Spielberg's famous film was based. Peter Carey has won many international awards – his book *Illywacker* tells the story of Australia in the early days of the twentieth century, not long after it had first become a united country. Today many people think Tim Winton – whose novels, including *The Turning* and *Cloudstreet*, have won many awards – is one of the most talented novelists around.

ART

Art, and especially painting, is one area in which Indigenous Australian culture has spread beyond the Aboriginal community. Indigenous Australian paintings are popular both within Australia and internationally, with artists such as Albert Namatjira and Emily Kngwarreye becoming well known around the world. The best-known non-Aboriginal artists are probably Sidney Nolan, Fred Williams and Russell Drysdale. The latter is famous for his pictures of the Outback.

▶ The author Thomas Keneally in the study of his Sydney northern beaches home in 2001.

FILM

At the start of the twentieth century, Australia was one of the first countries in the world to have a film industry. The industry died out during the 1920s and 1930s but has come back to life and now produces 20 or so feature films a year. Notable Australian directors include Peter Weir and Bruce Beresford. Australia is probably better known, however, as home to actors such as Russell Crowe, Nicole Kidman and Guy Pearce.

MUSIC AND THEATRE

Australia has national opera and ballet companies, and some big cities have their own orchestras and dance companies. State capitals also have their own theatre companies, and Australia's international theatre festivals are world famous. Australia's most famous popular music performer is probably the singer Kylie Minogue. Other successful international acts include bands like Silverchair and Powderfinger.

 Did you know?

Some people claim that an Australian film made in 1906 was the world's first feature film. Entitled *The Story of the Kelly Gang*, it was a six-minute fictional account of the Australian folk-hero, Ned Kelly.

SPORT

Sport is the glue that binds Australians, especially men, together. Whether playing as amateurs, or watching it being played by professionals, Australians take sport very seriously. For a country with a relatively small population, Australia is phenomenally successful at an incredible range of sports.

The country's most popular game is probably 'Aussie Rules' football, a tough game of

▼ The singer Kylie Minogue on stage in 2004.

kicking and punching or tapping an oval ball. There are 18 players on each team, and they aim to score points for 'goals', or 'behinds'. There is a big professional league, with teams coming from right across the country. At first difficult for non-Australians to understand, this tough, fast-moving game is nonetheless very exciting to watch.

The list of sports in which Australia has teams of competitors among the world's best is a long one. They include swimming, cricket, rugby union, rugby league, netball, cycling, hockey, surfing, motor racing (bikes and cars), cycling, tennis and athletics. The Socceroos, the national soccer team, reached the second round of the 2006 World Cup. Australia, with very limited snow sports facilities, has even managed to produce some excellent skiers and snowboarders.

 Did you know?

Almost seven million people went to see 'Aussie Rules' football matches in 2005.

Focus on: The Sydney Olympics

In 2000, Sydney hosted the Olympic Games. They were the most successful – or at least, the most watched – sports event in history. Roughly 3.7 billion people tuned in from 220 different countries and territories. Part of the reason for the success of the Games was the city of Sydney and its people. Many Sydneysiders volunteered to help make sure the huge numbers of athletes and visitors to the city had a good time. Sports-crazy Australians bought almost every available ticket: 92 per cent were sold, a huge improvement on the previous record of 82 per cent set by the Atlanta Games in 1996. Even traditional hard sells such as early rounds of the swimming found they were playing to full houses and, as a result, the athletes turned in some incredibly exciting performances. Many people agreed with the chairman of the International Olympic Committee when he said the Sydney Olympics were: 'The best Games ever.'

◀ A volleyball player 'digging' the ball at the 2000 Olympics in Sydney.

CHAPTER 12

Leisure and Tourism

Australians are fortunate enough to live in a warm, mainly dry climate. It is rarely very cold, and the coastal areas are only infrequently too hot. Australia is an easy place to spend a lot of time outdoors and, as a result, people have a real love of what is often called 'the outdoor life'. Australians in general love to socialize outdoors, and sport is an important part of this. Playing sports, cooking and eating outdoors, camping and spending time at the beach or in the countryside are all popular activities with many Australians. Walking in the 'bush' (wild scrub or forest lands) is increasingly popular, too, especially in spectacular locations such as the Blue Mountains.

THE BEACH

The beach is an important part of life for many Australians. With so many cities on or near the beaches, most Australians live within a relatively short journey of the seaside. They head for the beach on Sundays for family barbecues: many beaches have public grills, where a small amount of money in the slot buys you some cooking time. Nearby will be tables and chairs, some with shelter in case of wind or rain, where people can sit and eat what they have cooked. To prepare for a lifetime's

▼ A crowd watches a free Sunday concert outdoors in Melbourne in 2005.

obsession with another Australian pastime, surfing, many children also go to 'Little Nippers' surf lifesaving classes that are held on a number of beaches.

 Did you know?

Swimming in the sea on Sundays was illegal in Australia until the early twentieth century because it was considered immodest.

SURFING

Australia is home to some of the world's best surf breaks (recognized spots where people go surfing). Bell's Beach in Victoria, the giant surf of Margaret River in Western Australia, and the waves at Kirra on the west coast attract surfers from around the world. Almost every coastal settlement on the west, south or east coast has some sort of surf break. It is no wonder that Australia has produced some of the world's best surfers, including several world champions.

▼ A surfer rides the waves at Avalon Beach, New South Wales.

EATING OUT

'Barbies' are outdoor get-togethers based around cooking food on a barbecue. Guests often bring some food along, with everyone adding a little something to make a giant feast. To anyone not used to Aussie barbies, the large amounts of meat – burgers, sausages, chops and steaks – that get cooked and eaten can be amazing (and a little scary!).

Eating at restaurants is also popular, especially in the cities. Even here, people often take the chance to eat outside if they can. Australia is famous for its delicious 'fusion' cooking, which combines Western and Asian tastes.

MUSEUMS AND GALLERIES

Australia's bigger cities, in particular Melbourne, Sydney and Canberra, have excellent museums and art galleries. These mount permanent displays of their own, but they also often host visiting exhibitions from abroad. Many major travelling exhibitions of art make a stop in Australia.

TOURISM

Australia is a popular destination for international travellers. Most visitors come from New Zealand (21 per cent), Japan (15 per cent), the UK (14 per cent), the USA (9 per cent) and China (6 per cent). In addition, 23 per cent of visitors come from elsewhere in Asia, mainly South-east Asia, and 12 per cent come from mainland Europe. Australians also like to travel within their own country, and many tourists are from elsewhere in Australia.

Foreign travellers visit Australia for a variety of reasons: some for a holiday or to visit relatives, others for business or to work in Australia. The top ten activities for tourists include shopping, going to the beach (including swimming, surfing and diving) and visiting markets, pubs, clubs and discos. Tourists also visit national or state parks, wildlife parks, zoos and aquariums, botanical or other public gardens and may take a charter, cruise or ferry boat, visit heritage sites or monuments or take guided tours or excursions.

Sydney is by far the most popular place for tourists to visit, with over half of the visitors to Australia staying there for an average of 15 nights. The biggest attractions are the Opera House, the Sydney Harbour Bridge and the Darling Harbour complex of restaurants and shops. The most popular non-city areas are the tropical and semi-tropical parts of the east coast, in northern New South Wales and Queensland. Offshore here is the Great Barrier Reef (see page 5), which brings visiting divers and snorkellers from around the world.

Focus on: Environmental tourism

Many tourists come to experience Australia's natural environment, whether through a whale-watching trip, walking in the national parks, or some other activity. The number of such tourists has grown each year since 2000. In 2003, over 60 per cent of international visitors took part in activities that involved the environment.

◀ Tourists pose for a photo with the Opera House and Sydney Harbour Bridge in the background.

OTHER MAJOR ATTRACTIONS

Many people visit Australia without going to see particular attractions. However, the country is home to some incredible tourist sites, which draw in visitors from around the world.

Uluru, a giant rock formation in the desert at the centre of Australia (see page 15), has been used for years on posters for the Australian tourist industry. Almost every morning and evening, this site is busy with visitors. Other bush attractions include the Blue Mountains, west of Sydney, where spectacular rock escarpments and beautiful walking trails are popular with visitors. In Victoria, the Great Ocean Road winds alongside the sea on its way past the spectacular Twelve Apostles, a dramatic group of rock pillars that stand in the ocean.

▶ Tourists shackled together for a sightseeing tour of the Sydney Harbour Bridge. They are required to put on grey suits, which blend in with the bridge so that the views of it from elsewhere are not spoiled.

Did you know?

More than a million people have now climbed the Sydney Harbour Bridge.

Tourism in Australia

🗁 Tourist arrivals, millions: 5.215
🗁 Earnings from tourism in US$: 14,528,000,000
🗁 Tourism as % foreign earnings: 15.9
🗁 Tourist departures, millions: 3.388
🗁 Expenditure on tourism in US$: 10,136,000,512

Source: World Bank

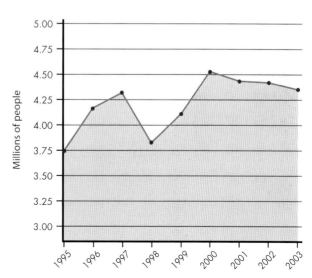

▲ Changes in international tourism, 1995-2003

CHAPTER 13

Environment and Conservation

Australia is home to a unique environment. Separated from other landmasses roughly 200 million years ago, its plants and animals developed to become completely different from those anywhere else in the world. There are thousands of species that exist in Australia and nowhere else. Australia's best known animals include kangaroos, koalas, echidnas, platypuses, cockatoos and emus. The country's distinctive plants and trees include eucalyptus trees and acacias.

A FRAGILE ECOSYSTEM

Australia's natural environment, particularly in areas with little rainfall, is fragile. It has developed in balance over vast stretches of time. Sudden changes of any kind put such a strain on the environment that it quickly reaches a breaking point. For example, wells for new houses can quickly exhaust underground water supplies that have nourished plants for thousands of years. Increases in population, including the numbers of tourists, are also putting the environment under increased strain. For example, areas like the Blue Mountains and the Great Barrier Reef are being damaged by the presence of tens of thousands of tourist visitors each year.

LOSS OF HABITAT

Of course, humans have been living in, and changing, the Australian environment for a long time. But all the major environmental changes have happened during the last 200 years or so, since the European settlers arrived. In the last 200 years, 40 per cent of all forests have been cleared and 70 per cent of all native vegetation has been lost.

The loss of these habitats has had a serious effect on the animals that adapted to them over millions of years. Another problem for native animals and plants is the introduction of new species from outside Australia. One example of this is the rabbit, which ruined crops and natural vegetation, depriving native species of

◀ Koalas live nowhere else on earth but Australia. Their diet is made up of eucalyptus leaves, so they can only survive where these trees grow.

food, before its numbers were brought under control. The combination of lost habitats and competition or hunting by new species has had a terrible effect on Australia's native species. Animals such as the tree kangaroo, the numbat, the greater bilby and the quoll are either extinct or on the verge of extinction.

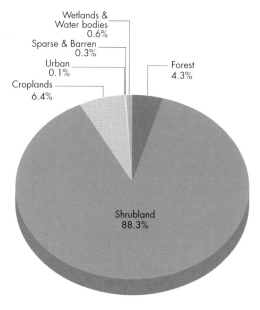

Wetlands &
Water bodies
0.6%

Sparse & Barren
0.3%

Urban
0.1%

Croplands
6.4%

Forest
4.3%

Shrubland
88.3%

▲ Habitat type as a percentage of total area

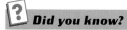

? Did you know?

Australia has lost 75 per cent of its rainforests in the last 200 years.

Focus on: Tasmania's forests

Tasmania has some of the oldest and tallest hardwood forests in Australia. These are a valuable resource, and logging companies have been removing the old-growth trees at a rate of about 20,000 hectares (49,420 acres) every year. Environmentalists are fighting a long, bitter campaign to save Tasmania's forests. They point out that, although the logging is profitable, it costs Tasmania dearly in other ways. For example, endangered species such as the Tasmanian wedge-tailed eagle, the giant freshwater crayfish (the world's largest) and the 'tiger cat' (or spotted-tail quoll) are losing their habitats. Also, the forests are not being replaced. Usually the logging companies create plantations of rows of new types of tree, to be cut down again in 15-20 years' time. The logging companies also use poison to clear the plantations of animals that would eat young saplings, and the poison indiscriminately kills anything coming into contact with it.

▼ In the state of Victoria a rainstorm waters an area of pastureland that has been cleared for agricultural use.

SUSTAINABILITY

'Sustainability' describes using natural resources in a way that will mean other people can still enjoy them in the future. For example, the city of Sydney currently uses water at a rate of 108 per cent of its water resources. For every 10 litres of water available from rainfall, rivers and other sources, 10.8 litres get used. This is unsustainable: at some point, if things continue like this, Sydney's water reserves will be used up.

Australians live unsustainable lifestyles in many ways. One example is that they are using the continent's supplies of groundwater at a far faster rate than they are being replaced. All those showers, swimming pools, flushing toilets and other high-water-use activities come at a cost to the environment. Few people are willing to give them up, however – despite the fact that the water will one day run out if it continues to be used at the same rate as today, even though there is no projected date by when this might happen.

WASTE

Australians are among the most wasteful people on earth, in the amount of actual waste they create per person. The only country more wasteful than Australia is the USA. More than 18 million tonnes of household waste are sent to Australian landfill sites each year. One calculation says that this is enough waste to cover the entire state of Victoria in a layer of waste 100mm deep. At some point, Victoria's landfill – a waste mountain – will become visible over the horizon.

KYOTO PROTOCOL

In 1997, many of the world's nations signed up to the Kyoto Protocol on Climate Change. This aimed to reduce the amount of greenhouse gases released into the environment, with each country setting a target for how much their

▼ Australia's high levels of water use – for example, in private swimming pools – will not be sustainable in the future.

greenhouse emissions would change. Most wealthy countries aimed to reduce their emissions, but Australia insisted on being allowed to increase its emissions by 8 per cent, and did not sign up to the protocol.

POSITIVE NEWS

Despite all this, Australia was ranked thirteenth in the world in the 2005 Environmental Sustainability Index. In 1999, the Environment Protection and Biodiversity Conservation Act, which aims to protect threatened species, became law. National and state parks offer some protection to Australia's unique ecosystems; 64 wetlands are registered under the Ramsar Convention, and 16 world heritage sites have been established.

On a personal level, many Australians are trying to live in a more sustainable way, especially in less built-up areas. Composting toilets are increasingly popular, and solar panels or windmills provide power. In the cities, many people are trying to reduce their dependence on cars. State governments are insisting that new buildings use less energy and are sited near public transport, so that car use decreases.

Organizations such as the Australian Conservation Foundation, the Wilderness Society and the Australian Trust for Conservation Volunteers work on projects aimed at protecting Australia's environment. Visitors to Australia can now choose to go WWOOFing, as part of the Willing Workers On Organic Farms scheme.

Environmental and conservation data

- Forested area as % total land area: 4.3
- Protected area as % total land area: 7.5
- Number of protected areas: 4,487

SPECIES DIVERSITY

Category	Known species	Threatened species
Mammals	252	63
Breeding birds	497	37
Reptiles	876	38
Amphibians	228	35
Fish	1,489	44
Plants	15,638	38

Source: World Resources Institute

▶ The Bungle Bungles are a maze of narrow gorges and secluded gullies, accessible to eco-tourists by walking tracks, and are rich in Aboriginal culture and history.

CHAPTER 14

Future Challenges

What does the future hold for Australia? On the positive side, the country has a number of advantages. It produces nearly all its own food, so does not have to rely on imports to feed its people. It is blessed with a number of valuable natural resources, in some of which it is the world leader. If, as fossil fuels run out, the world becomes more dependent on nuclear power, Australia's extensive uranium deposits will become increasingly valuable.

MAINTAINING TOLERANCE

Australia has largely been able to accept immigrants without the problems of ghettoization and resentment that have resulted from large scale immigration in other countries. Australia is generally a tolerant and friendly place, though at times there have been conflicts between Australian-born and immigrant communities. In 2005, for example, there were clashes on Sydney's southern beaches between white Australians and Lebanese-Australians.

Australia does face a number of major challenges in the future, however. Among these are the economy, the situation of Indigenous Australian people, the environment and the threat of terrorism.

▼ In 2005, Olympic gold medallist Cathy Freeman (on the left) takes part in the 'Long Walk', a march to protest the rights of Indigenous Australian people.

THE ECONOMY

Australia is a wealthy country with a strong economy. However, many exports are raw materials such as iron, coal or food animals. These exports are vulnerable to competition from elsewhere in the world, and their value is affected by prices on world commodity markets. Meanwhile, many imports are of high-value manufactured goods, which are more expensive in relative terms. The government is trying to encourage a growth in the production and export of manufactured goods, rather than raw materials, to bring the country more income.

INDIGENOUS AUSTRALIANS

Indigenous Australians have the lowest standard of living of any group in Australian society. Australia likes to see itself as a fair society, but the situation of its original inhabitants argues that this is not always the case.

THE ENVIRONMENT

Australia does not exist in a sustainable way. In such a fragile environment this could be disastrous, first for the plants and animals of the continent, then for its people. A particular challenge is to persuade people to give up some of the creature comforts that make life in the sometimes harsh environment more pleasant.

TERRORISM

Australia's international actions, especially its support for US foreign policies and its role in East Timor, have made it a target for terrorist attacks by Islamic extremists. The attacks in Bali in 2002 and 2005, for example, were aimed largely at Western tourists, most of them Australians. Australia will need to adopt international policies and security measures to prevent further terrorist attacks.

▼ Enjoying life outdoors: joggers in Sydney, with the main business district and botanical gardens in the background.

Timeline

200 million years ago The Australian continent breaks away, as the earth's continents slowly move apart. From this time on, Australia is an isolated landmass.

40-60,000 years ago The first humans arrive in Australia from Asia.

1606 The Dutch navigator, Willem Jansz, makes the first confirmed sighting of Australia.

1642-3 The Dutch navigator, Abel Tasman, sails round Australia without sighting the mainland. He discovers Tasmania, which he names 'Van Diemen's Land'.

1688 Former buccaneer William Dampier lands on Australia's north-west coast, somewhere around King Sound in what is now Western Australia. He records what he sees in a journal.

1770 British Navy captain, James Cook, sights and explores the fertile east coast of Australia. This is the first time that Europeans have seen the land as anything other than dry, barren and largely valueless. Cook claims the land for Britain and names it New South Wales.

1787 Captain Arthur Phillip – with 570 male and 160 female convicts, about 200 British soldiers, about 30 wives of soldiers and a few children – sets sail for New South Wales to establish a prison colony. The group travels in 11 ships. The first ship reaches Botany Bay, on Australia's east coast, on 18 January 1788. Phillip's ship arrives on 19 January, and the rest arrive on 20 January. The colony's first settlement is near a large harbour about 11 km (7 miles) north of Botany Bay, the current site of the city of Sydney.

1790s The British colonial government gives military officers and freed convicts permission to settle lands in Australia.

1803-63 Various further settlements and territories are established, including Melbourne in the 1830s.

1851 Gold is discovered in New South Wales and then in Victoria. Australia's population soars – from about 400,000 in 1850 to more than 1,100,000 in 1860. Most of the newcomers arrive during the Gold Rush.

1860 Burke and Wills lead an expedition across the interior. Both men die on the return journey from the north coast.

1868 The practice of sending convicts to Australia is ended. More than 160,000 people had been transported by that time.

1899-1902 Australian armed forces are involved in fighting, on behalf of the British, in the Boer War in South Africa.

1901 The Commonwealth of Australia is formed; it is the first time Australia has been a united country.

1914-18 Thousands of Australian men travel to Europe to fight in the First World War.

1939-45 Australia fights in Europe and Asia-Pacific during the Second World War. More than 29,000 Australian service people are killed.

1950-3 Australian troops are involved, in support of the USA, in the war in Korea.

1964 Conscription is introduced in Australia. Young Australian men are sent to fight in the Vietnam War, in support of the USA.

1967 Prime Minister Harold Holt disappears while swimming in the sea near Melbourne. At the height of the Cold War, rumours abound that Holt has been abducted by the crew of a Chinese submarine. Later it is revealed that Holt has, in fact, drowned.

1972 Australia's relations with the USA become strained as Australian troops are brought home from the Vietnam War.

1975 A crisis occurs when the British Queen's unelected representative in Australia, Governor General Sir John Kerr, removes the democratically elected prime minister, Gough Whitlam.

1990s Prime Minister Paul Keating recommends that Australia cuts its ties with Britain and becomes a republic.

1999 In a referendum upon whether they want their country to remain a constitutional monarchy or to become a republic, the Australian people decide to keep the monarchy. Australia leads an international force to help the territory of East Timor become independent from Indonesia.

2001 Australia supports the US-led invasion of Afghanistan.

2002 A bomb attack by Muslim terrorists in Kuta on the Indonesian island of Bali claims the lives of 89 Australians.

2003 Australia supports the US-led invasion of Iraq.

Glossary

Animal husbandry The practice of farming animals.

ANZUS A defence agreement signed between Australia, New Zealand and the USA in 1951, agreeing that an attack on one country would represent an assault on all three.

Arable Capable of being used for growing crops.

Arid Particularly dry. Technically, 'arid' describes an area with less than 25 cm (10 in) of rain each year.

Capital Wealth in the form of property or money; often used to describe money available for investment.

Cold War The state of hostility between the USA and USSR between approximately 1948 and 1990.

Colonial Relating to, or belonging to a colony.

Colony A country under the political control of another country and occupied by people from that country.

Commonwealth The name for the federated Australian states.

Communism An economic system in which the means of production, distribution and exchange are controlled by the state.

Communist A follower of communism.

Conscription Forcing people to join the armed forces for a set period of time.

Constitutional monarchy A system of government in which the head of state is the king or queen, but power is held by an elected body.

Crust The earth's crust is its hard outer layer.

Diggers Australian soldiers, many of whom took part in the First World War. They are greatly revered by their fellow Australians. Some people say they were known as 'diggers' because many of them had once been gold miners. Others say it was because of their trench-digging activities during the war.

Ecosystem A group of plants and animals that depend on one another and the land they live in to survive.

Eucalyptus Tall, evergreen trees that grown mainly in Australia.

Federation The government of a large area, which has been formed by an alliance between smaller states or territories. The states or territories may have some degree of independence in their internal affairs.

Free trade Trade between countries or territories without any taxes on the goods that go from one to another.

Geologists People who study landforms.

Ghettoization The creation of communities of people who are isolated from the rest of society. These communities are usually poor.

Gross Domestic Product (GDP) Total value of goods and services produced within the borders of a country.

Gross National Income (GNI) Total value of a country's income from goods and services produced by its residents both within the country and elsewhere in the world.

Groundwater Water held underground in natural reservoirs.

Irrigation The use of water supplied by artificial routes to help crops grow.

Kinship group A group of people who recognize that they are all related to one another.

Militia A military group raised from the general population to assist the army in an emergency; or a rebel group acting in opposition to the regular army.

Ochre An earthy yellow-orange colour.

Opal A semi-precious stone found in large quantities in Australia.

Plateau A high, flat area of land.

Referendum A vote among a group of people about a single issue.

Republic A country with an elected head of state and elected representatives.

SEATO An anti-communist alliance between Australia and several other Western and Asian countries. SEATO was dissolved in 1977.

Southern Hemisphere The area of the earth south of the equator, the imaginary line that goes around the middle of the planet.

Sustainable Capable of being maintained or repeated.

Tsunami A series of giant, fast-moving surges caused by an undersea earthquake, landslide or volcanic eruption.

USSR The Union of Soviet Socialist Republics, a giant, powerful country formed in 1922. From 1945, the USSR rivalled the USA as a major world power, but it disintegrated in around 1989. Today's Russia was the largest of the USSR's constituent parts.

Vocational Describes education that will train someone for a particular job or career, such as plumbing, engineering or journalism.

WWOOF A scheme that provides opportunities for people to work on organic farms, donating their time to projects they feel do not damage the environment.

Further Information

BOOKS TO READ

Global Cities: Sydney
Paul Mason
(Evans Brothers, 2006)
A detailed look at one of Australia's most
important cities, including information on its
history, people and culture.

Nations of the World: Australia
Robert Darlington
(Raintree, 2004)
This book has lots of information on how
Indigenous Australians and more recent
immigrants have interacted over the years.

World Tour: Australia
(Raintree, 2004)
Explores Australia through the imaginary
scrapbook of a tourist visiting the country.

Destination Detectives: Australia
Miriam Lumb
(Raintree, 2006)
Explores Australia through the eyes of a traveller
who mysteriously wakes up there one morning.

Continents: Australia and Oceania
(Heinemann Library, 2006)
Places Australia in the context of the Pacific
region, giving information on people and culture.

All About Continents: Australia and Antarctica
Bruce McLeish
(Heinemann Library, 2004)
With information on Australia and Antarctica,
the uninhabited continent explorers were
searching for when they first sighted Australia.

*Continents of the World: Australia, Oceania and
Antarctica*
Kate Darian-Smith
(Hodder Wayland, 2005)
The history, landscape, economy and people.

The Changing Face of Australia
Margot Richardson
(Hodder Wayland, 2005)
The ways in which Australia has been changed
by its immigrants since the Second World War,
and the different people living in Australia today.

USEFUL WEBSITES

www.abs.gov.au
The home page for the Australian Bureau of
statistics with detailed information about almost
every aspect of life in Australia.

www.dpmc.gov.au
The Department of the prime minister and
Cabinet: has information about almost every
aspect of Australian life that is affected by
government policy. Also has useful links, to
sites such as the Council of Australian
Governments, a forum for national, state and
territory governments to discuss issues.

www.tourism.australia.com
Information about many aspects of the tourism
industry in Australia.

www.wilderness.org.au
The home page of one of Australia's
environmental campaign groups.

Index

Page numbers in **bold** indicate pictures.

About the Author

Otto James divides his time between writing for books and websites and travelling. He writes mainly about travel, geography and sports.

Otto's favourite places in Australia are the First Drop Café in Sydney and Airey's Inlet, along Victoria's Great Ocean Road.